THE HEALING HEART

THE HEALING HEART

POEMS OF LOSS AND LIFE

ELEANOR KOLDOFSKY

MALCOLM LESTER BOOKS

Canadian Cataloguing in Publication Data

Koldofsky, Eleanor, 1920–
    The healing heart : poems of loss and life

ISBN 1-894121-02-3

I. Title.

PS8571.0689H42 1998   C811'.54   C98-930159-1
PR9199.3.K633H42 1998

Design: Tania Craan
Typesetting: Jean Lightfoot Peters

Malcolm Lester Books
25 Isabella Street
Toronto, Ontario
M4Y 1M7

Printed and bound in Canada
98 99 00 5 4 3 2 1

to Barbara Bondar
without whom this book
would never have come to be

CONTENTS

PREFACE

I have written these poems touching on anger, grief, pain, regret, memories, emptiness. All these words, if put together, would make a tome too heavy to carry.

Yet, we all carry memories, like a never-ending pregnancy. What is to become of this sorrow forever-attached?

It must be alchemized to strengthen our resources so we can be more for others.

Yes, pain will be felt in our hearts, etched on our faces...but our mind must be exempt...for the next blow.

THE HEALING HEART

ROOM 1642

I hear the voice of Ferrier.
I see the dance of Fonteyn
as I approach your bed.
I know that you, as they,
have become a legend
for the beauty you bestowed
on the world.

And your reward:
The smiling face of bone
ever grimacing
always waiting
smothering life's fulfillment
with mutilation
cancer
radiation—
not the illumination of one's achievement.

But of tissue and sinew
how long will this continue?
Loved ones hold their breath
in dread, in fear, in terror,
always on the verge of tears.

The wards are filled
as You hang
on your crossed sticks
in your modest loin cloth
beguiling us
into a religion
as though You
were the only crucifixion.

One on the wall.
One on the bed.

(*in memory of actress Yvette Brind'Amour*)

VORTEX

The vortex spins you around.
The silent screams well up—
you're drowning.

But you have to surface.

Spend each waking minute
thinking of one person.

You have to surface.

And it's hard.

NONE OF IT WAS AN ACCIDENT

My mind is a graveyard of wreckage,
memories of style, years, models,
all used, rusted.
Dials without control
wheels that cannot turn
brakes, seized, burned
windscreen, shattered
open to every storm
steering column awry
headlights that warned—now dead
no gauges to guide, protection stilled
motor unmotivated.

All wasted, ugly, useless
waiting for the next head-on.

PAIN

You will hurt.
You will hurt so much
you can't believe
your life is so painfilled.
That which was so pure
can turn
destroy
betray
kill.
Yet you will survive.

CONCEALMENT

Do you know how level
I kept myself
terrified you too would injure yourself?
How I could not share grief
because of two invalids
who needed caring,
nurturing, healing?
Where were my needs?
My grief, my sorrow
hidden behind an apron,
a stove, a meal.
No time to share the truth.

LISTEN

Hear the scream of the hunted man
in days bygone.
Hear the terror of the children
deformed for gain.

Hear the cries of injustice
as weighted trees
creak and groan
burdens of men swaying.

Hear the weeping of millions
packed in trains speeding
to their deaths.
Hear the children snuffling.
Death awaiting.

All these little starvelings
innocent
wondering
hungry
they are so silent.

Their screams resound in my head.

TODAY

My thoughts are raw and sore,
there isn't much to give a damn about any more
though,
should tomorrow come
and to those I love bring pain,
how glad I would be
to have this day again.

RITUAL

I am in a bed.
Instant adjustment.

Dread.

Recognition.

What is this day?
I must figure a way
to find
in my mind
what day this is
and why it is
I do not want to.

So terrible.

I know
I must rise and go.
Meticulously, I dress. I prepare,
but slow with care
not to rush, don't push myself.

I remember when he did push
and came out fine.
It was a happy time.
Strong and lovely with a sturdy arched back,
proud was I just to lie back.
Eyes pure brown, hair so black,
square little shoulders,
smooth satin limbs,
all things right in this tiny him.

The doctor declared,
He's a real little whopper
with a tiny cock
and a wee clapper.
And grow did he
so did we
bursting with pride
at the length
of his stride
and his smile and his call.

Time went ahead in leaps and bounds.
He could pick me up and swing me 'round.

It was so good.
It was life's food.
If not that what else?

I must comb my hair
and take some tea
or what will there be left of me.
I shall slip on a coat.

The clouds are racing.
The winds are soughing.
Slow as I have been, I must be going,
the fear in me rising and growing.

Every sense batted down, smothered.
Keep it down. Be strong for others.

Your mind goes ahead
and you've descended the stairs.

That you've managed so far
no one cares.

Time is passing
for what and for whom?
My time is through.
But it's not—
would that it were.

There are others to be living for.

With all eyes upon you
you are indifferent.
You attend the service
hear words intermittent.

By and large
it was a good sermon
soon, not soon enough,
to be forgotten.

Nothing nothing nothing
will return my son.

NIGHTS

My nights are stronger than my days.
A night will release thoughts inhibited all day
and resolutely come to a conclusion.
Not that I sleep, although why shouldn't I?
The brain will continue to collect, collate, correct,
create new material to hide upon awakening,
perhaps through the day an inkling,
a remembrance, a little dance of thought.

The days you get through.

The nights get through you.

LIVING

If living is hurting I'm living.
If living is loving I'm living I'm loving.
If living is hating and fearing and sharing
and a vortex of pain and despairing
I'm living.

KITING

If I am ever blind
take me to an open beach
where I can run
and feel the sun
and let the wind
blow through my hollow eyes
to ease the pain
of never seeing you again.

If that were all,
mind kiting free,
with what ease
take we our burdens
to the seas.

WHO WILL BE THE ONE?

Who will be the one to find me dead?
Who will be the one to hold my head,
to close my eyes, without surprise
to know the inevitable
that my life was full?

LAMENT

What did you leave when you left me?
What will there be
that won't start its decay,
to linger until the day
when numbness subsides
and the real pain begins.
And abides.

HOUSEKEEPING

If I am a building
am I made of stone, of brick, wood,
    glass, metal?
What shape do I take?
Am I tall or wide?
How many rooms—how large?
How deep are my cellars?
What lives in my attics?

If I did a drawing of me
what would I see?
Some people say I am beautiful.
What do they see?
I must have windows
    into which they peer.

I am inside
housekeeping
    quietly mopping up tears.

CAVERNOUS LOSSES

My grief is a pit
a Grand Canyon reservoir.
I never knew its depths
until I began to fill it.
Is there any bottom
any sounding place?

At first the tears fall deeply
soundlessly.

A plumb swinging freely
not finding the rest
and then it lands
lies crooked for a while
slowly rights itself.
I am a fixed line of grief.

The next time
my tears
travel directly
down this line
but never again
reach
bottom.

PIETÀS

The world is filled with grieving Pietàs—
lovers holding broken bodies in their arms
looking out despairingly
to be free from suffering,
their deserved right.
We watch them dying.
We bless, applaud,
urge the girding of their innermost desires
to assuage the pain of their departure.

We lose one.
They lose everyone.
Searching into eyes for their last flicker
a gleam of pure love.
Releasing hands
beloved fingers once strong, demanding.
Now.
Someone hovering.
Waiting.
Impatient.

How does Death prepare for so many artists?
We are hardly prepared for one.

(*in memory of film critic Jay Scott*)

FRAGMENTS I

The layers of consciousness are
stripped away
impaling her to another day.

*

She went probing for Grief and discovered
Shame
caused by Grief's absence.

*

Sad poets live in secret places
that hurt all the time.
She lived where all the sad poets live.

DOROTHY

I

When we were small
and you were bigger
you cared for me
my Champion.
You braved all the dragons.
You were my wall
my comfort.

Now we are bigger
and you are hurt
I would come to you
and cradle you
and free you from your pain.

But once again
God loves the same people I do.

II

In my mind
I pluck an entire ginkgo tree
bringing it to you,
each Egyptian fan-like leaf
cooling your fevered brow.

In my mind
I carry you in my arms
into fields of English daffodils
where your entire being
will sense a kingdom
effortless in dance.
My strength for your freedom.

In my mind
I hold you close and safe
always in my heart,
your calm and surest place
to revel in all things free and fair.

III

I saw someone today
who looked like you.
The same noble head
listening to the music,
the brows arching
over her fine brown eyes,
fingers softly tapping concert time.

My heart leapt
with pleasure and pain.
So good to see again,
the smile around your lips
as you listened to the song.

I did not know how much I ached to see you.
You have been dead so long.

(*in memory of my sister*)

RESONANCE

Death is always sudden.
However long one vigils
when it comes
the quiet report it sounds
in your head
reverberates for years
with pain
and loss
and longing.

SHELL GAME

Pain is something you don't feel
when something is hurting you more.
The heart is sore
the mind won't surface.
Does each and every test
have to be taken in one exam
sorted out like different shells, strung
in the mind—fluttering?
Different hells,
picked and chosen,
which is first, which is worse
too many from which to choose.

Choose all, choose none.
You lose.

MARGARET

You lived to give
breath and life
the spirit of music
the wealth of it
to children.

You spent your life
in this pursuit.
Now
your reward—
unremitting pain
death.

I look at you and wonder
at the inestimable knowledge
stored in your brain
and beseech
you to call
this lodestone
of memory
to use.

The music,
poetry, philosophy
of Sartre, Isherwood,
Picasso, Schumann
Rorem—the innumerable
comforts, loves and inspirators
of your history.

Think! Concentrate!
I implore you—to bring
you back from pain, to hearing
their poems and music
that you know
intrinsically
will metamorphose your mind.

Pain will flee.
You will have
conquered the agony of death
and calmly depart
still in noble dignity.

(*in memory of Margaret Butler*)

THE MAGIC MAN

If I were a magic man,
"With all the power invested in me"
(as they say)
"and could erase your memories…"

And I remember how my son thrived—
what he ate, how he loved to pitch
that fast ball with such direction.
The swimmer who could go for miles.
The shy smile that slid like
a raindrop down a petal,
you had to catch it or miss it.
The strength in the young arms
surprising from behind crushing me.
The questions, "Mom, you're singing a sad song,
    are you sad?
I thought singing was happy."
He taught me.

There is so much intimacy with
your children that seems casual.
When you know everything about them
then they die.

And the magic man said,
"If I could remove all these memories
and your pain in his untimely death,
would you want that?"

What a foolish question.

VACANCY

The deepest pain
is the absence of it
after all the years
of nurturing each shared moment.
And now, the non-igniting memories.

Memory
wondering
at the meandering intermezzo of life
no longer sailing on the breeze,
now a preserved thistle
captured in dullness to stay
refracting loneliness day by day.

ACCEPTANCE

You cry a lot
and then you don't cry anymore.
You hurt a lot
then you don't hurt anymore.
You sit and look at the waste,
a basin of sand
after the tide goes out
leaving all its irregularities.

Are you just the next thing
to get over?

FRAGMENTS II

Deep in my heart
a grave lies
taking over
where no comfort can reside.
You who have loved me so dearly
how can you take my life
by losing yours?

*

Minds need not be torn
to suffer and rend
a love we know will not end.

*

I remember every room
that we were ever in.
Now I am aware
of every room
where you are not.

*

The utter confusion
to which my life was thrown
can not be borne.

     *

I am somewhere that you never were
and I am lost.
Even were I somewhere that you were
and you not there
I could find some comfort.

     *

The recollection of happiness
is not happiness.
The recollection of pain
Is Pain itself.

SEARCHING

I'm not hurting as much today
as I did yesterday.
But I can't be sure of tomorrow.
When you have searched eyes
in which all doors stand opened
each door exposing
depths,
regions one doesn't know exist,
you come to the end of things in yourself.

EMPTINESS

Everything I want to say
has been said by someone else.
Everything I want to use
is up there on the shelf
of my imagination
and there is nowhere else to search.

I am so barren.
There is no one for whom I long
no place
no favorite song.

In the lapse
the collapse of all.

DEPTHS

How many levels does life hold?
How many plateaus?
How many depths?
How joyous that I have lived on each with you
barring the one to which I descend
when you are gone.

DREDGING

When I was a child
my mother was neither caring nor nurturing.
I was there
and when there was food
I got some.
When there wasn't
I held my cheeks in my hands
while she went off to other lands,
spending her time in cinemas,
cleansing her sorrows with fantasy enemas,
purging her hunger and cold.
Abandonment and derision,
her only decision
living in the land of the rich and pampered,
heedless of her children,
spending all day and evening as well
before another night of living hell.

DUTY

When my mother was alive,
as a child
I neither loved nor admired her
though I cared and respected her.
And as a child did abide
the life that she led and was living
Hell would describe.

As I grew, and did with my own cares collide
my attachment to her was lassoed
not by an umbilical cord
but rather an electric coil—a line
responding to each whimper and whine,
my every thought, feeling, imagined neglect,
shrouded with guilt.
I had no love, no return, no affection,
a life of emotional dereliction.

My life was not a desert.
A desert has an oasis.

BOBBY

You lived in my body
nourished and loved
swam lazily
daily caressed
intravenessed
stretching and turning
bubbled and burped
as I lay on my back
occasionally heartburning
until you were forced out.

You lived in my house
growing and learning
playing and hurting
ribalding and sibalding
ruled and schooled
taught and caught
fed and bed.

Then you moved out.

PROGENY

I once imagined I was a mother
with fine young sons
and more than that
grandsons
to frolic with and play
cuddle and treat
love and hug
wait to meet
live the dreams
that mothers have.

I had them
and nothing like that happened.

GOODBYE

When a mother
abandons her children,
it's a disgrace
a crime.

When children
abandon their mother,
they're just free
having a good time.

They'll look down and say,
"How're feeling?"
I'll say,
"I am feeling.
But not for long.
How about you?"

DECOMPOSE

Wilting for lack of affection
as a child unflowering
as a wife uncherished
as a lover unwanted
as lonely as a new cemetery.

Isolated bouquets

planted far apart.

WASTE

I am an emotional desert.
I am dry, used by years of restraint,
disallowing feeling,
mind careening,
pitted by
the erosion of mistrust.

Where is the anger that will cleanse?
When does it come?
Why wait for the years
tumbling carelessly by?
Renew life, try,
fight, scream, make it known:
It is famine to be alone.

CONTACT

I waited so many years
silent
bearing the burden of abandonment
waiting for a sign
so the years would not
reflect on them.
Waiting for a time
when a genuine act of love,
one word, one touch,
would make me forget
the exile
and the world would think
nothing happened.

ON GUARD

I'm afraid of love.
I'm afraid of the pain
afraid of the loss
and of the forever game.
I walk to a rhythm of
a secret not guessed
with grace and dignity
and unremitting emptiness.

MUSING

Sometimes in my mind
I say things aloud,
sometimes louder than others.
Then I hear them
and they resound
in that cramped cavern
echoing in that visceral cavity,
vibrations telegraphed to no one.

LAST GRACE

Listen my dear,
She is old and in pain.
She lives through the night
to another day
worse than the night before.
Let her go sooner.

Don't have regrets.

WHEN?

Have I hurt enough
to have learned anything?

I am not beautiful
(now and then there are flashes)
but when I was,
I didn't know it anyway.

CUMULATE

Too many hair shirts
hanging in my cupboard
taking up headspace.
leaving me no place.

Don't have to count them,
itemize
realize
all of that before part
a duty imposed
an exercise of will.

AMUSEMENT PARK

I've listened to the calliope
walking through the crowd
the hawkers crying out their wares
children shrieking joy aloud
sidesaddled on the carousel
going round and round and round
missing the ring
too many times.

NO OFFICIAL EXISTENCE

Looking back over the years of my life
I fit into a mosaic,
a picture I don't want to see
of all the mistakes that were me.

FRAGMENTS III

Our ever insufficient knowledge
of the future
is it called hope or fear?

*

The instant crippling of the mind:
Striding by a reflecting window
eyes turned to find
lithe, slim, youth
has changed into
me.

*

It is no longer the seasons changing.
It's my life passing.

*

Sometimes I am afraid of my own blood
pulsing through my arteries
like the dull thud of footsteps
in the silence of the night.

*

Circuits of fear
penetrate deeper recesses
of composure
durability.

*

To relive this day
with all the happiness I failed to see.

ONE MORE THING TO FORGET

One more thing to forget,
a small kitten has died.
One more thing to forget,
a mutilated bird
lying on its side.
One more thing to forget,
that I am hollow inside
now that you have left me.
One more thing to forget,
that life goes on they say.
One more thing to forget,
tomorrow is another day.
One more thing to forget,
my entire life gets in the way
when you're not with me.

CONVALESCENT

I walk the streets in quest of you
searching every face
remembering.
Needing different words
to describe
how much we meant to each other.
How impossible without you!
How many years will it take to recover?

LOVE

Love is all that matters
Not love of God.
Not love of children.
Childbirth?
Fulfillment—overrated!
Love of self?
Love of art—music?
None of these.

Love of another,
a physical interplay
of mind, heart, body—and sometimes soul.

This is the whole.
The rest is detritus.

Some who have truly loved know this.

SYLVIA

Your love was showered on me like confetti
and where they landed in profusion on my life
left a shaft of color bright.

(*in memory of my sister-in-law*)

FRAGMENTS IV

The wells of love
filling from springs of the past
freshets of pain, pleasure, failures.

*

My forehead in anguish
leaning on the window
looking in.

*

If we only had the capacity
to stop loving when it hurts.
What have we as an alternative?

*

I have built a shield of autonomy
integrity complete
unviolated
impervious
safe
even from love.

REMEMBERING

Gold torn from fingers
necklaces warmed on the throat
a fob recalling a costume
pieces of the past
treasures of loved ones
lost.

Once proud adornments
remains of love or wealth
boxed in secret places
I light upon,
my eyes brimming
remember ring.

HOPPER

We have a storage bin of memories,
treasures that remind one
of a place, a lover, a day
to relive and return,
to look at, to hold
feel them warm still,
we know we never will.
A rock, some sand, ringlets of hair,
the rare bits of time,
the sight of them our personal
archeology
restructuring the past.

TEA PARTY

My grandson
whom I had not seen
for a very long time
met me at the door
and he was only two.

We hugged and kissed
and whirled about
filling the room
with shrieks and shouts,
my darling Jhase and me.

Weary with playing hockey
he invited me to tea.

He took my hand
and up we climbed
the stairs to his very own room.
Set the cups and saucers
creamer, sugar and pot
we were enjoying this a lot
nor did we forget spoons.

Everything on his toy table
as we sat on his tiny chairs.
He graciously poured
into two little cups
and we helped ourselves to air,
my darling Jhase and me.

Laughter and smiles
of great approval
exchanged to the very last drop.
Another cup, Grandma?
Oh, so filled, it was time to stop.
His velvet brown eyes
and shyness,
his slow smile at my pleasure
made it for me always
the best tea party ever.
And we were only two.

WEIGHTS AND MEASURES

The measure of love
is not loss.
It is, though,
giving, taking,
sharing, understanding,
hoping,
sexual loving—feeling, hands,
fingers, tongues,
strong arms, legs
wrestling softly,
caressing,
loving deeply.

Remembering
is the measure.

DEATH

In each land
on many grassy plains
or knolls
decorated all
a cemetery.

And in each one
my son lies.

Wherever I pass
under a plot of grass or snow
my son lies, he cannot grow.

Only in my thoughts.

Stones cannot bury him
nor frozen fields.
Life has forsaken him.
Death will not yield
this stripling youth
who lived in me.

Who lives in me.

SIBLINGS

He was your brother
(he was my son first).
We waited five years for you
and you were all the brother and son
we needed.
You grew under his tutelage.
He taught you all he knew
and learned more
to be more
for you.

METE

Her life
and her death
collided in her
bloodied cough
death won
again.

But her life will live
in everyone's heart.
We will banish death
believing we
for a little while
have conquered time.

FRAGMENTS V

I have a hole in my memory that bleeds.
Why, when the itch of that healing scab forms,
do I tear it off?
Am I not living now
that I must remember when I did?

*

However I think
whatever I hope
as free as I could be
I tithe to the past,
never absolved.
My freedom, onerously taxed
for reasons unknown.
The tithing continues.

*

Which memory shall I choose tonight
until I fall asleep?
What have I sown
that now I may reap?
The joys that were best
were to last my life through.
Where are you?
Where are you?

ICE CREAM

The ice cream from my cone
is lying on the street—at my feet
like my love,
no way to recover, put back into shape
melting away from me.
What a treasure it was.

BOUQUET

I must stop visiting graves.
Graves of people
sons, mothers, sisters, brothers, friends.
Graves of buried achievements, of losses, of hope
graves of pride
graves of ideas.

Let them die
in their too early demise.

I will leave yet another bouquet
and rise
and be on my way.

HISTORY

My history is not a pretty picture.
The futile sifting,
trying to find what is made up
of myself.
The swinging memories, pivoting,
refracting gallows each with its own
hanged guilt.
Rappelling, crashing against the rugged crag of
    truth,
not always a welcome visitor.
More a visitation,
an affliction.
Every attempt must be made
to climb, face the rugged cliff
of years.
I hold on with bloodied fingers
to the truth.

FRAGMENTS VI

I intellectualize my emotions
turning them into shrapnel
pitting and scarring
my behaviour.
I sear my mind with thoughts
that cauterize the wounds
that time has wrought
of man's indifference.

*

If I wasn't a woman
and had stored up all my tears
I would have been
drowned by now.

*

I do not intend to grow older
repeating the same stupid mistakes.
We all believe we are going through doors
to new things.
I have been going through kitchen doors.

*

From first to last
it remains the same.
Life has only one age
the eternal youth of the soul.

CHOICES?

Do I want to die neat
with my money all spent
and no chores to be done
and not owing any rent
with my clothing all used?
To have said all goodbyes
and to some with relief
no longer joys and sighs.
No, I want to live on
to love, laugh and sing
to be frozen in winter
and breathe again of sweet spring.
To be utterly happy
mind running free
able to give more of what's me.
To have worked all my life
and fought for every breath
now do I cease
and come to terms with death?

LESSON

Teach me not to covet.
Teach me to find strengths in my own
    existentialism
my great responsibility to self.
Teach me the gift of rage.
Show me for what I worked
not knowing this passion constantly lurked.
Let go this patronage.
Identify this intimate carnage.

PENCIL BOX

I started off life wanting a pencil box
with secret drawers.
All of my prayers
for one little box
to store my pencils and pens
to write my thoughts and dreams.

I climbed my first mountain
and the box obtained
then for another mountain searched again.
More elaborate cupboards and shelves
to accumulate the parts of myself
to costume the charade
my daily parade
of theater, concert music and entertainment.
I forgot whatever sane meant.
My life progresses
I want less and less.
My childish drawers
now filled with horrors
now looking for a pencil with a point
to end my talk
before the final box.

CERTAINTY

To become myself
I am trying out selves
to have a core of self certainty
conviction.
My years have revealed pentimento.
My mother's youngest
my husband's adornment
my children's all-need-appliance
my lover's pain.

I now have a center.
I will be what I want to be.

SUMMING UP

I did exactly what I wanted to do with my life.
It does not matter how it adds up
because
I'm always beginning.
I'm doing what I'm supposed to do.

Years enlarge.

My birthdays
are not regressive days.

PASSION

I am older and the flames do not leap as high,
though I smolder
waiting for your breath
to pass by,
flaming the coals.

RENASCENT

I am borne in the arms of love
floating in the care and minds
of friends bearing my burdens
seemingly weightlessly.

Before
my pride would have
none of it.

Now Pride sits—
washed—combed—
waiting for the healing.